Poland

Sean McCollum

🌿 Carolrhoda Books, Inc. / Minneapolis

Photo Acknowledgments

Photographs, maps, and artworks are used courtesy of: John Erste, pp. 1, 2–3, 20, 23, 28–29, 30, 33, 40, 42; Laura Westlund, pp. 5, 11, 31; © Witold Skrypczak/Tom Stack & Associates, pp. 4, 6, 7, 9 (top), 15, 21, 24, 26 (both), 27; © Jakub Jasinski/Visuals Unlimited, p. 8; © **TRIP**/(TH Foto-Werbung), pp. 9 (bottom), 22, (A. Tovy), p. 14, (W. Jacobs), pp. 16, 37, (P. Petterson), p. 17, (Z. Harasym), pp. 18, 25 (top), (A. Gasson), p. 31, (C. Rennie), p. 44; Basilica of the National Shrine of the Immaculate Conception, Washington, D.C., p. 10; © Elaine Little/World Photo Images, p. 12; Reuters/Corbis-Bettmann, pp. 13, 19; © Michael Philip Manheim/Photo Network, p. 25 (bottom); IPS, p. 28; © János Kalmár, pp. 32, 38, 39, 40, 43; **Panos Pictures** (© Jeremy Hartley), pp. 34, 35 (both), (© Chris Sattlberger), p. 36 (both); © Bryan Ney, p. 41; © A.J.Copley/Visuals Unlimited, p. 44. Cover photo of a village church near the Carpathian Mountains © Witold Skrypczak/Tom Stack & Associates.

Carolrhoda Books, Inc.
A Division of the Lerner Publishing Group
241 First Avenue North
Minneapolis, Minnesota 55401 U.S.A.

Website address: www.lernerbooks.com

Words in **bold type** are explained in a glossary that begins on page 44.

Library of Congress Cataloging-in-Publication Data

McCollum, Sean.
    Poland / by Sean McCollum
        p.   cm. — (Globe-trotters club)
    Includes index.
    Summary: Examines the geography, history, economy, society, and culture of Poland
    ISBN 1–57505–106–0 (lib.bdg. : alk. paper)
    Poland—Juvenile literature. [1. Poland.] I. Title II. Series:
Globe-trotters club (Series)
DK4147.M39 1999
843.8—dc21   98–8831

Manufactured in the United States of America
1 2 3 4 5 6 – JR – 04 03 02 01 00 99

Contents

Witamy w **Polsce!***

That's "Welcome to Poland" in Polish, the official language of Poland.

Poland sits in the north central part of the continent of Europe. On the map, the country sort of looks like a lion's head with a shaggy mane. (The lion's nose touches Lithuania.) The Baltic Sea laps against the shores of northern Poland. A little bit of Russia, most of which is farther east, meets the rest of Poland's northern edge. Then, moving clockwise, you'll come upon Lithuania to the northeast of Poland. Belarus and Ukraine share Poland's eastern side. Two mountain ranges—the Carpathian in the southeast and the Sudety in the southwest—separate Poland from its southern neighbors, Slovakia and the Czech Republic. Germany lies to the west.

The city of Torun lies on the Vistula River.

Following the **Vistula**

Paths in the high, jagged Tatra Mountains (part of the Carpathians) are popular with Polish hikers.

 To see much of Poland's landscape, follow the course of the Vistula River, the nation's longest waterway. The journey begins among the Carpathian Mountains in southwestern Poland. The national parks in this forested region are favorite spots for Poles to hike and pitch tents. Many people in the Carpathians work in the lumber industry, and trucks loaded with huge logs rumble toward the mills.

The mountains give way to a small but crowded area known as the Polish Uplands. Farmers plant crops in the rich soil. A lot of the people who live in the uplands work deep underground in coal mines.

Fast Facts about Poland

Name: Rzeczpospolita Polska (Republic of Poland)
Area: 120,756 square miles
Main Landforms: Central Plains, Carpathian Mountains, Sudety Mountains, Masurian Lakes, Vistula River, Oder River
Highest Point: Rysy Peak (8,197 feet)
Lowest Point: Below sea level

Animals: Eagle, wild pig, stork, wolf, fox, brown bear, European bison, tarpan (wild horse), lynx, elk, swan, eel
Capital City: Warsaw
Other Major Cities: Łódź, Kraków, Wrocław, Poznań, Gdańsk
Official Language: Polish
Money Unit: Złoty

Farmers mow a green field near a village in the Polish Uplands.

7

Keep Heading
North

 The land flattens out as the Vistula River winds through the Central **Plains,** which dominate most of Poland. Hang on to your hat—wind sweeps across this open farmland! Harvests from the fields of wheat, rye, and potatoes make their way to the tables of Polish families.

In the Lake Region, the land becomes hilly and wooded—just the ticket for Poles who love the outdoors. Glaciers (gigantic sheets of ice) once covered the area. Thousands of years ago, they pushed up the ground into small, rocky hills and dug the pits that have become the nation's thousands of lakes.

Tidy fields of crops ripen in the sunshine of the Central Plains.

The Vistula splits the Lake Region in two. The part that spreads over northeastern Poland is the Masurian Lakes. The Pomeranian Lakes fill the nation's northwestern corner.

The Vistula continues northward toward the Gulf of Gdańsk, part of the Baltic Sea. At the shore are the Coastal Lowlands. This narrow band contains the only section of Poland that dips below sea level. Then it's sand dunes and beaches. *Splash*! Welcome to the Baltic Sea.

Children on vacation in the Masurian Lakes region investigate the water with a stick (above). **Bathers enjoy a sunny day on a Baltic Sea beach** (left).

9

Polish **Roots**

Poles are a Slavic people who are related to Russians, Czechs, Bulgarians, and many other **ethnic groups** in central, eastern, and southern Europe. People within an ethnic group share a religion, a history, and a language. Some linguists (people who study languages) believe that more than 5,000 years ago, Slavs lived as a single group. Their clue is that the many modern-day Slavic languages contain similar words and ways of making sentences.

Around A.D. 200, the Slavs broke into three main branches—East Slavs, South Slavs, and West Slavs. About 20 communities of one group of West Slavs were known as the Polanie, "people of the plains." They settled in the valleys of the Vistula and Oder Rivers. These long-ago Slavs are the **ancestors** of modern-day Poles. In the 800s,

Poles mark the birth of their nation in 966, the date that Mieszko I (center) was baptized (accepted as a member) in the Roman Catholic Church.

the Polanie communities united to fight invaders, but they didn't yet have an official country. Poles mark 966—when the Polanie ruler Prince Mieszko I accepted Roman Catholicism as the religion of the people—as the year their ancestors founded Poland.

Home of the White Eagle

A famous Polish legend claims that a group led by three brothers—Rus, Czech, and Lech—wandered in to a beautiful, green land. Lech saw a white eagle building a nest and thought this was a sign that they should stay. But Rus and Czech wanted to keep going, so the group split into three parts. Guess where Rus went—yep, Russia! And what about Czech? The Czech Republic. Lech stayed in what would become Poland, and the white eagle on a red background is still a symbol of the nation. The same colors appear on the Polish flag.

Very Polish
Poland

Because most Poles share
the same ethnic background,
people who aren't related
still might look alike.

Why do many Poles have fair skin and brown hair, although in a lot of other countries, one person will look very different from the next? As a group, Poles look similar because around 97 percent of the nation's almost 39 million people are **ethnic Poles.** The other 3 percent have German, Ukrainian, and Belarussian backgrounds. These folks work hard to keep their cultural traditions alive.

But Poland hasn't always been so Polish. Before World War II (1939–1945), Poland was home to about three million Jews. In 1939 Germany invaded Poland. Adolf Hitler, leader of a German group called the Nazis, blamed Jews for many of his nation's troubles. Hitler's goals included wiping out Polish culture and Europe's Jews. The Nazis set up **concentration camps,** where millions of people were killed. All but 250,000 Polish Jews died in the war, and many who survived moved out of Poland. About 10,000 Jews remain in Poland.

The numbers of Germans and Ukrainians in Poland also shrank. Some of these people didn't move. Poland's postwar boundaries were redrawn. The citizens ended up being part of neighboring countries.

During World War II, Nazi Germany imprisoned many people in buildings such as this one at Auschwitz, Poland. These days the concentration camp at Auschwitz stands as a reminder of the war and of the people who died.

Toughing It **Out**

Poles live in a tough area of Europe, where struggles over land have been frequent. And Poland has had a difficult time defending its territory. In fact, the nation was wiped off the map from 1795 to 1918, when Russia, Prussia (a former Germanic kingdom), and Austria divided Polish territory.

Poland suffered another blow during World War II, when Germany took over the country. Six million Poles died, and the fighting destroyed many Polish cities.

After the war, the **Communist** Party ruled Poland. Most Poles objected to life under the rigid rules of Communism. They lost the rights to

Poles gathered in 1990, shortly after they voted in new leaders, to demonstrate support for Poland's non-Communist government.

The Good and the Bad

The good news is that southern Poland's soil contains lots of minerals. In fact, Poland has about 10 percent of all the world's coal. That's the bad news, too.

Poland's Communist government built many factories to produce energy and goods from the nation's natural resources. The bad part is that the government didn't update its industries with new ways to control pollution. Poland's soil, water, and air have been filled with poisons, harming many Poles' health.

In 1989, when Poland's government changed, many people wanted to clean up the country right away. But reducing pollution may mean putting lots of people out of work. Helping the environment while keeping Poles employed will be a hard balancing act.

A Polish boy peers from the window of this aged, weather-beaten farmhouse.

speak freely, to travel, and to follow their religion. They also endured shortages of food and supplies. In 1989 Poles regained the power to vote in non-Communist leaders. But life in Poland is still pretty tough.

Lunchtime brings citizens to an open-air café in Warsaw's Old Town.

Warsaw Rubble
Raisers

About a thousand years ago, Warsaw was a small settlement on the Vistula River. But in 1596, Poland's king made Warsaw the capital, and things really started cooking. These days more than 1.5 million people live in Warsaw, the nation's largest city, which sprawls over both riverbanks.

On the eastern side of Warsaw are tall apartment buildings and factories where most city dwellers live and work. Across the river is Old Town, which was almost completely destroyed during World War II. Poles love their capital and wanted it to look as it had for centuries. They used paintings and original blueprints to recreate many of its historic buildings, including a castle that had originally been built in the 1300s.

Warsaw's New Town *is* newer than Old Town—but not by much. The scent of pastries and rye bread drifts from the bakeries. Yum! Poles walk arm in arm, window-shopping or buying ice cream and bouquets at the stalls that line the square.

Horse-drawn carriages rattle and clop down this New Town street.

Polish Catholic kids dress up to celebrate their First Communions.

Catholic
Country

On Sunday mornings all over Poland, the streets are bustling with people on their way to Mass, the religious service of Roman Catholics. That's not the only clue that religion plays an important part in Polish everyday life. Pictures of the Virgin Mary (the mother of Jesus) or of the pope (the head of the Roman Catholic Church) hang in many Polish living rooms. Country folks often mark roads with religious statues or chapels. Church steeples dot city skylines. Children take religion classes in public schools. Married couples seldom divorce in Poland because the practice is against the teachings of the church.

Some 96 percent of Polish people belong to the Roman Catholic Church.

By the age of eight or nine, Polish Catholics receive First Communion. First Communion is an important event! It means that, for the first time, Catholic kids are allowed to participate in all parts of the church service. Relatives travel long distances for the big family celebration that follows the ceremony.

A small number of Polish Christians are not Roman Catholic. Instead they are members of the Eastern Orthodox or of a number of different Protestant churches.

Pope John Paul II

Polish Catholics hold a special affection for Pope John Paul II, who is not only the spiritual leader of Roman Catholics worldwide but is Polish. In 1978 the church selected Cardinal Karol Wojtyła to be pope. Wojtyła—who then changed his name—left Poland for Vatican City (Catholic headquarters) in Italy. The religious leader inspired his fellow Poles to continue challenging Communist rule, and he brought international attention to the Poles' political struggle.

Shweet **Zounds**

The sound of two Poles talking might sound like whispering—even if they're talking loudly! That's because Polish words have lots of "sh," "ch," and "z" sounds.

Some letters in Polish words have hooks underneath them or accents or dots over the top. Some Polish words, like *słyszeć* (hear) have the letter *ł*. This letter represents a sound similar to *w* in English.

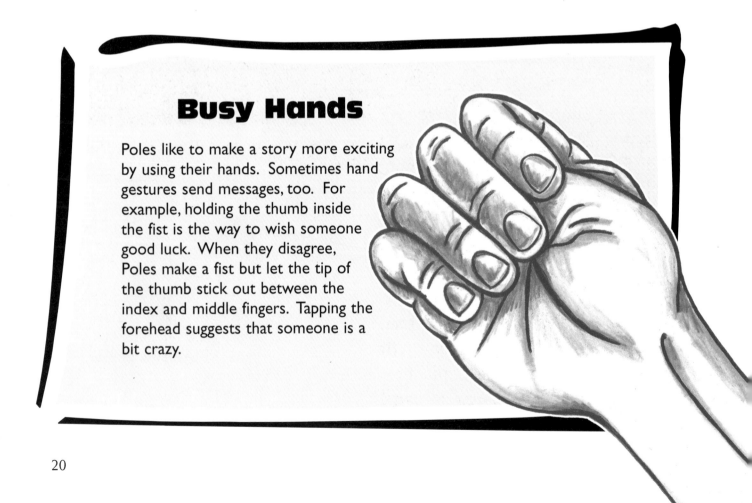

Busy Hands

Poles like to make a story more exciting by using their hands. Sometimes hand gestures send messages, too. For example, holding the thumb inside the fist is the way to wish someone good luck. When they disagree, Poles make a fist but let the tip of the thumb stick out between the index and middle fingers. Tapping the forehead suggests that someone is a bit crazy.

In different parts of Poland, people speak Polish slightly differently. These three friends live near Germany. Their Polish sounds a little like German!

Most Polish words look very different than English words do, but a few are close enough to English to be recognized. See if you can figure out what *telefon*, *plastyk*, *komputer*, *guma*, and *festival jazzowy* mean. (If you guessed "telephone," "plastic," "computer," "chewing gum," and "jazz festival," you're right!)

Home **Base**

Lots of city dwellers live in high-rise apartment buildings.

Two out of three Poles make their homes in cities such as Warsaw, Łódź, Kraków, or Gdańsk. City kids usually live in large apartment buildings. Many buildings date from the 1940s and 1950s, when millions of Polish people moved from the countryside to the cities to work in new factories. The government had to provide shelter for the new city dwellers. But Communist leaders focused on supplying housing as quickly and cheaply as possible rather than on making the apartment buildings beautiful or comfortable.

If you visit a Polish friend's home, you might be surprised the family can fit into the small living area. A typical apartment has two rooms—one bedroom and a living room with a cooking area tucked into the corner. Two or three families might share a restroom located off a central hallway.

Down on the
Farm

Some Polish farmers harvest their crops using age-old methods.

Have you heard the expression "time stood still," which means that things don't seem to change? In some parts of the Polish countryside, farm families live and work in much the same way as their long-ago relatives did. They pile hay on a wagon with pitchforks and then harness the wagon to a horse to take the hay to town.

About one of four Poles farms the land. A typical farm grows potatoes, sugar beets, cabbage, and grains, especially barley, rye, and wheat. Kids help take care of the family's pigs, cattle, and sheep.

Rural Poles have long celebrated the change of seasons. On the first day of spring, they drown Marzanna, a scarecrow that represents winter.

Girls dress in traditional costumes and hold pigeons as part of an autumn harvest festival.

August and September bring harvest festivals, when Poles give thanks for the crops. Big parades make their way from farm to farm. An altar boy leads the way, followed by the local priest, choirboys, and finally the church members. At each farm, a girl wearing a traditional regional costume presents a harvest wreath woven from heads of grain. The next spring, for good luck, the farmer will plant the seeds from the wreath first.

Zalipie House Painting

In rural Poland, spring cleaning and painting is a big tradition. The women in the village of Zalipie go all-out. One woman may paint a flower garden on the walls of her family's cottage, while her neighbor creates a patchwork of diamonds and squares on the house, the well, the barn, and even the doghouse! In June judges cast their votes for the most colorful creation.

In a house in the country, Polish kids have room to relax.

Family **Life**

What are Polish families like? In the countryside, families are large. But lots of city kids have just one brother or sister or are only children. Both parents work six days a week, and women do most of the housework.

All in the Family

Here are the Polish words for family members. Practice using these terms on your own family. See if they can understand you!

grandfather	dziadek	(JAH-dek)
grandmother	babcia	(BAHB-chah)
father	ojciec	(OY-chets)
mother	matka	(MAHT-kah)
uncle (father's brother)	stryj	(STREE-ee)
uncle (mother's brother)	wuj	(VOO-ee)
aunt	ciotka	(CHAHT-kah)
son	syn	(SIHN)
daughter	córka	(TSOOR-kah)
brother	brat	(BRAHT)
sister	siostra	(SHOH-strah)

A family crowds around the table for tea and a light snack.

Whether in the city or the countryside, Sundays are for family get-togethers. After Mass, grandparents, aunts, uncles, and cousins, if they live nearby, gather in a relative's home. Some kids see their cousins only on important occasions, like First Communions, weddings, or funerals. It's common for relatives to live near one another in the country. Sometimes they even share the same house.

Some family members might discuss an upcoming soccer tournament. Others help in the kitchen. Trays of food appear on the lace-covered table. Then the family gathers around the table to eat and chat.

A big, steaming bowl of bigos tastes great for dinner!

Barszcz, Bigos, and
Berry
Bombs!

Polish cooks have a saying: *Gość w dom, Bóg w dom*. That means "A guest in the home is God in the home." You'll be fed well if you're invited to a Polish house for dinner.

The first course may be dark rye bread with a steaming bowl of *barszcz*, a rich soup made from beets. Then the host might serve *śledź w śmietanie*, a mixture of herring and onions in sour cream. Biting into a pierogi (dumpling) is always a pleasant surprise. Cooks stuff the dough with cheese, sauerkraut (pickled cabbage), or meat.

Don't fill up yet—Poland's national dish, *bigos*, is next. In this stew, you'll find chunks of bacon or sausage, fresh cabbage, and sauerkraut flavored with herbs. Cooks usually make the stew ahead of time because bigos gets better every time it's reheated. To eat like a Pole, dip spoonfuls of bigos in horseradish. Hooeey—no more stuffy nose!

How about dessert? Ice cream and poppy-seed cake are big hits at Polish tables.

Berry Bomb

You will need:

2 cups berries (raspberries,
   strawberries, or blueberries)

2 cups heavy whipping cream
2 cups sugar

Wash the berries thoroughly. (If using frozen berries, thaw the fruit.) Put them in a blender. Purée the berries until they are liquid. Set aside. Pour the cream into a large bowl. Add the sugar gradually as you whip the cream with a hand mixer. Slowly stir in the berries. Put the mixture into the freezer. After 90 minutes, remove the bowl from the freezer and stir again. Pour the berries into a mold or a serving bowl. Return the mixture to the freezer and wait 2 more hours before digging in. Serves 6.

Celebrating the
Polish Way

Poles know how to stretch out holidays. Christmas and Easter mean the most to Poland's Catholics. Christmas Eve is a favorite time for Polish kids. They keep a lookout for the first star. When it appears, each family member gets a thin wafer called an *opłatek*. They break off and eat bits of one another's wafers as they exchange wishes for good luck in the coming year. Then the family shares *wigilia*—Christmas Eve dinner. A layer of straw under the white tablecloth reminds them of Jesus in the manger. After the meal, the group sings carols. Kids have one eye on the Christmas tree, because exchanging presents comes next.

Poles go all out when they make *pisanki* (Easter eggs), which, according to folklore, bring good health

Happy Name Day to You!

In Poland, you'd be disappointed if you expected a big birthday bash. Except for the little kids, Poles celebrate their name day instead. Catholics are often named after saints, and each Catholic saint has a feast day. Families of boys named after Saint Nicholas, for example, throw a party for their Nicholas on December 6—Saint Nicholas Day.

Friends surprise one another with buckets of water on Easter Monday. Everyone gets wet!

and a plentiful harvest. These many-colored eggs are decorated with fancy patterns. On the day before Easter, Poles take the pisanki to church—along with food for Easter dinner—for the priest's blessing. All seriousness is forgotten on Śmigus Dingus Day, Easter Monday. Boys sneak up to dump buckets of water on girls. But the girls know what to expect and are prepared with buckets of their own. Gotcha!

Dear Grandma,
Last night, June 23, was Midsummer's Eve. The part I liked best was an old tradition. All over Poland, young women floated wreaths and candles on tiny rafts. Each man grabbed one raft. If the fellow whom a woman likes chooses hers, they might marry. Poles say they don't really believe this, but lots of candles twinkled on the river.

See you soon!
Janie

31

Making the
Grade

Students on a field trip hike through a national park.

"Knowledge is the key to power" is a saying Polish grown-ups are fond of repeating. Poles think it's important to get a good education, and Polish kids are often several years ahead of North American students in their studies. Youngsters begin school when they're seven. During the eight years of elementary school, students take classes in science, math, history, geography, Polish, literature, and social studies. Some schools hold computer science and

Schooltime

Polish kids take off their street shoes and change into slippers to help keep the floors of their schools clean. The school gives each student a number, and sometimes the teachers call on kids using numbers rather than names.

foreign language classes after the regular schoolday ends. Teachers assign lots of homework. Polish kids go to school six days a week from September to mid-June. The schoolday usually starts at eight or nine o'clock in the morning and ends by one or two o'clock.

After completing eighth grade, Polish teens have finished their required schooling, but most Poles continue their education. Their interests and their test scores determine what they'll study in high school.

The Białowieża Forest is one of the largest remaining wooded areas in Europe.

Poland's Time
Machine

Polish city kids on a school field trip might feel like they have stepped back in time when their class visits the Białowieża Forest, near where Poland meets Belarus. In times of old, the ruling class held this land as a private hunting ground. Logging wasn't allowed, so some of these trees have been growing for hundreds of years!

Bison

Europeans almost hunted the **bison**—the continent's largest animal—to extinction. But in 1921, the Polish government set up its first national park in the Białowieźa Forest. These days about 1,600 bison roam through the trees. And bison are just one of 3,000 types of animals that call this park home.

Imagine riding with classmates in horse-drawn carts along narrow, dimly lit trails. The tops of the towering trees soar as high as 15-story buildings! In one patch of trees, kids learn Polish history at the same time as they enjoy nature. Each of the trees in Royal Oaks Way is named after a person from Poland's long-ago royalty.

A cartload of kids ends a tour through the forest.

Lots to **See**

Poles enjoy celebrating their culture and history and sharing them with others. The country has many museums and interesting sights. Want to visit a museum in a salt mine?

The fancy St. Kinga Chapel wasn't built— it was hollowed out of the Wieliczka salt mine! Nearby stand life-sized statues carved from the glittering, gray salt (inset).

These days the only "monsters" at Wawel Castle in Kraków are the big fish that this angler hopes to pull from the Vistula.

Deep underground at Wieliczka, where salt miners have dug out the salt for a thousand years, workers have also created huge chapels with altars, pictures, chandeliers, hand railings, and stairs carved from salt. Step inside another chamber to see the salt gnomes (dwarfs).

Wawel Hill in Kraków gives a sense of long-ago Poland. Kings lived in Wawel Castle, and they were buried at the cathedral on the hill. Legend has it that a dragon once lived beneath the castle. A man named Krak killed the dragon and saved the city.

Warsaw has all kinds of museums. The Poster Museum displays the work of Polish artists known worldwide. At the National Museum, the paintings of Jan Matejko, who lived in the 1800s, show scenes and famous people from Polish history. At the Ethnographic Museum, colorful Polish costumes, tapestries, wood carvings, and paintings fill the rooms.

Book **Lovers**

A reader relaxes with his novel near the steps of Kraków's city hall.

A walk through a Polish city will reveal how much Poles love to read. At an outdoor café, a woman might hold a book while sipping tea. A group of teenagers at another table may be having a lively discussion about an article in the newspaper. On pleasant days, booksellers set tables loaded with books on the sidewalks. Even when they're in a hurry, Poles will have a hard time passing by without browsing. And the public libraries are packed.

written down—they were long poems to be sung or spoken.

Poles are great writers, too. Each year one writer worldwide is awarded the Nobel Prize in literature. Five Polish authors have won this great honor during the 1900s. Polish poetry and novels can be sad, because writers often describe the courage Poles have needed to overcome the nation's troubles. In fact, a lot of writers had to leave Poland to write. Isaac Bashevis Singer, a Polish Jew, moved to the United States and wrote many Jewish legends. His children's story *The Golem* is based on a Jewish legend of a monster that protects Jews.

Shoppers stop to look at a bookseller's outdoor table.

Land of **Music**

A young Pole plays his saxophone at an outdoor concert.

Fiddles, accordions, horns, flutes, and bagpipes join together to make the bouncy oom-pah-pah of Polish folk tunes. Have you ever danced the polka? Southern Poles may have been the first to ever play this lively music. Polish weddings or folk-music festivals feature many types of traditional Polish music, including tunes written for the mazurka and the polonaise—Poland's national dances.

For hundreds of years, Poles in regional costumes have twirled or danced in lines. Long-ago musicians wrote music that went along with the swirling of women's flowered skirts and the stomping of men's boots.

These dances inspired Poland's best-known composer (music writer) and pianist, Frédéric Chopin. By the mid-nineteenth century, his love of Polish folk music had worked its way into his piano compositions. Musicians worldwide still play Chopin's music, which means that lots of people have heard Polish rhythms.

Every five years, the world's top pianists participate in Warsaw's International Chopin Competition. Other Polish cities also host classical, jazz, opera, and Polish folk festivals.

Polish kids are likely to listen to pop, rock, and rap music. Some bands have even combined the sounds of Polish folk music and reggae!

Street musicians play traditional Polish tunes for passersby.

Time Out

Most Polish workers get four weeks of vacation a year. If the family wants an outdoor adventure, they may take a train to the mountains. Skiing doesn't get much better than in Zakopane, a favorite vacation spot in the Tatra Mountains.

Polish kids think sleigh rides are great fun. A thick blanket keeps everyone cozy as the horse pulls the sleigh through the countryside. At the end of the ride, groups gather at a bonfire to eat and dance as musicians play folk songs.

After the snow melts, hikers take to the trails. Poles who enjoy the water have lots of choices. Some people climb aboard the rafts on the Dunajec River in southern Poland. Wearing a regional costume, a guide steers the raft and tells Polish legends. Cottages in the Lake Region fill up with families who fish and canoe. Along the Baltic coast, people enjoy the beaches and resorts.

Families may visit historic places or go to music festivals. They buy souvenirs, such as carved wooden plates or *wycinanki*—paper cutouts in the shapes of animals or flowers.

Storytelling guides steer a boat full of Polish vacationers down the Dunajec River.

Glossary

ancestor: A relative in the past, such as a great-great grandparent.

bison: A wild animal of the ox family. The American bison is often known as the buffalo.

Communism: A system of government in which the state (rather than private individuals) owns and controls all farms, factories, and businesses.

concentration camp: A prison camp that confines people who are believed to be dangerous to the group that runs the government.

Holy Smoke

In August thousands of Polish Catholics walk long distances to the Jasna Góra Monastery in south central Poland to honor a painting called the Black Madonna. So named because the paint has darkened from age and candle smoke, the picture is said to have healing powers. According to legends, the painting has caused invading armies to turn back.

Creepy Crawler Jewelry

Folks dipping nets along the coast of the Baltic Sea aren't scooping fish. They're pulling amber from the shallow water. Amber is the hardened sap of pine trees that grew near the Baltic Sea millions of years ago. Poles shape these yellowish orange chunks into settings of silver that's been mined in Poland, creating beautiful jewelry. Some pieces of amber preserve prehistoric insects that were caught in the sticky material before it became solid. Jeepers creepers!

ethnic group: A large community of people that shares a number of social features in common such as language, religion, or customs.

ethnic Pole: A descendant of an early West Slavic people called the Polanie who make up the largest ethnic group in Poland.

plain: A broad, flat area of land that has few trees or other outstanding natural features.

Pronunciation Guide

barszcz	BURSHCH
Białowieża	bee-yah-lah-vee-YEHZ-yah
Carpathian	kahr-PAY-thee-ehn
Czech	CHEHK
Dunajec	doo-NAH-yehts
Frédéric Chopin	FREE-deh-rihk SHOH-pan
Gdańsk	geh-DAHNSK
Gość w dom, Bóg w dom	GOSH vah DOHM, BOOG vah DOHM
Jan Matejko	YAHN mah-TYEH-koh
Karol Wojtyła	CAHR-ohl voyt-YEH-lah
Kraków:	KRAH-kahw
Lech	LYEHK
Łódź	WOOCH
opłatek	oh-PLAH-tehk
pierniki	peer-NEE-kee
pierogi	pee-ROH-gee
pisanki	pee-SUHN-kee
Rzeczpospolita Polska	zhech-pahs-pah-LEE-tuh POHL-skuh
śledź w śmietanie	SHLEDGE vah shmeh-TAH-nyah
słyszeć	SWISH-ehtz
Śmigus-Dingus	SHMIH-goos DIHN-goos
Sudeten	soo-DAY-ten
Vistula	VISH-choo-lah
Wawel	VAH-vuhl
Wieliczka	vyeh-LEECH-kah
wigilia	vee-GHEE-lyah
Witamy w Polsce	vee-TAH-mee vah POHLS-tzah
wycinanki	vee-tzee-NAHN-kee
Zakopane	zuh-kah-PUH-neh
Zalipie	ZAH-leep-yeh
złoty	ZLAH-tee

Further Reading

Donica, Ewa. *We Live in Poland*. Charlottesville, VA: Bookwright Press, 1985.

Drucker, Malka. *Jacob's Rescue: A Holocaust Story*. New York: Bantam Books, 1993.

Heale, Jay. *Poland*. North Bellmore, NY: Marshall Cavendish, 1994.

Heinberg, Richard. *Celebrate the Solstice: Honoring the Earth's Seasonal Rhythms through Festival and Ceremony*. Wheaton, IL: Quest Books, 1993.

Hintz, Martin. *Poland*. New York: Children's Press, 1998.

Knab, Sophie. *Polish Customs, Traditions, and Folklore*. New York: Hippocrene Books, 1996.

Lazo, Caroline. *Lech Walesa*. New York: Dillon Press, 1993.

Otfinoski, Steven. *Poland*. New York: Facts on File, 1995.

Poland in Pictures. Minneapolis: Lerner Publications Company, 1994.

Roberts, Jack. *Oskar Schindler*. San Diego: Lucent Books, 1996.

Singer, Isaac Bashevis. *When Shlemiel Went to Warsaw and Other Stories*. New York: Farrar, Straus and Giroux, 1986.

Skipper, G. C. *Invasion of Poland*. Danbury, CT: Children's Press, 1983.

Zamojska-Hutchins, Danuta. *Cooking the Polish Way*. Minneapolis: Lerner Publications Company, 1984.

Metric Conversion Chart

WHEN YOU KNOW:	MULTIPLY BY:	TO FIND:
teaspoon	5.0	milliliters
Tablespoon	15.0	milliliters
cup	0.24	liters
inches	2.54	centimeters
feet	0.3048	meters
miles	1.609	kilometers
square miles	2.59	square kilometers
degrees Fahrenheit	5/9 (after subtracting 32)	degrees Celsius

Index